YOUR KNOWLEDGE HAS VALUE

Bibliographic information published by the German National Library:

The German National Library lists this publication in the National Bibliography; detailed bibliographic data are available on the Internet at http://dnb.dnb.de .

Imprint:

Copyright © 2014 GRIN Verlag, Open Publishing GmbH
Print and binding: Books on Demand GmbH, Norderstedt Germany
ISBN: 9783668471177

This book at GRIN:

http://www.grin.com/en/e-book/369514/advantages-and-drawbacks-of-gesture-based-interaction

Andrea Attwenger

Advantages and Drawbacks of Gesture-based Interaction

GRIN Publishing

GRIN - Your knowledge has value

Since its foundation in 1998, GRIN has specialized in publishing academic texts by students, college teachers and other academics as e-book and printed book. The website www.grin.com is an ideal platform for presenting term papers, final papers, scientific essays, dissertations and specialist books.

Visit us on the internet:

http://www.grin.com/

http://www.facebook.com/grincom

http://www.twitter.com/grin_com

Andrea Attwenger
Proseminar Media Informatics
Department of Computer Science
University of Munich, Germany
summer 2014

Proseminar Media Informatics

Advantages and Drawbacks
of Gesture-Based Interaction

Abstract:

With the increasing prevalence of smartphones, gesture-based interaction has arrived in our everyday life, but we still do not exploit its full potential. This paper describes the benefits and drawbacks of gestural input and presents interaction techniques that address these drawbacks.

Gestures provide the user with a new form of interaction that mirrors their experience in the real world. They feel natural and require neither interruption nor an additional device. Furthermore, they do not limit the user to a single point of input, but instead offer various forms of interaction.

However, gestures also raise issues that are not relevant with traditional methods of input. The need to be learned and remembered, which requires the development of guides that promote the discoverability and memorability of these gestures and deal with input and recognition errors. Another aspect is the design of the gestures itself, which should make them memorable and easy and comfortable to execute.

Keywords:

gesture; guide; learnability; gesture design; memorability; gesture recognition

Inhaltsverzeichnis

1. Introduction

In the last few years, gesture-controlled interactive surfaces have become widespread. Since natural human communication consists mainly of voice, facial expressions and gestures, it is only logical that developers try to imitate that behaviour in their interfaces.

2. Advantages

The desktop computing paradigm limits the users' flexibility by forcing them to interact using a 2-Degree-Of-Freedom device (the mouse), while they are used to interacting with the physical world in much more differentiated ways (Bellucci, Malizia & Aedo, 2014). Gestures allow the user to handle multiple points of input and even define several parameters at once. They are, therefore, a more natural form of communication.

2.1 Immediate and powerful interaction

Unlike traditional buttons and menus, gestures do not interrupt the user's activity by forcing him to move his hand to the location of a command. Instead, they can be performed directly from the current cursor position. (Bau & Mackay, 2008)

Also, they do not require any additional devices: the command and even its parameters can be specified by a simple hand movement (Baudel & Beaudouin-Lafon, 1993). Input devices narrow down the user's possibilities of interaction, for example a pen or a mouse limiting the potential forms of input to single-touch interaction. Gestures that are performed with the user's hands however, can be versatile and do not have these constraints. As Wobbrock et al. put it: "almost anything one can do with one's hands could be a potential gesture" (Wobbrock, Morris & Wilson, 2009). This includes not only the movement or the followed path of the hand, but the movement and position of every finger as well as the general hand posture. (Brandl, Forlines, Wigdor, Haller & Shen, 2008)

2.2 Intuitiveness and enjoyability

Gestures feel very natural to perform since they mirror our experiences in the real world. Maybe that is the reason a study by Watson et al. showed that participants using touch-input for a task were enjoying themselves more and also felt more competent compared to participants using a mouse. They systematically favoured direct touch input over mouse input and also performed better regarding speed and accuracy. (Watson, Hancock,

Mandryk & Birk, 2013)

In addition, Cao, Ofek and Vronay found that gesture-controlled presentations were not only perceived as more enjoyable by the presenter but also as more attractive by the audience. The presenters were able to make eye contact more often and to use their body language to convey information. (2005)

3. Drawbacks and possible solutions

Gesture-based interfaces have many advantages and provide the user with a completely new form of interaction. However, this kind of input also raises issues that are not relevant with traditional input. On the user's side, these problems are to learn, to remember and to accurately execute gestures. The developer has to provide a system that correctly recognizes these gestures. Freeman et al. remarked that the observation of gestures does not suffice in order to learn them, as the observer is unable to differentiate relevant and irrelevant movements. (Freeman, Benko, Morris & Wigdor, 2009) Therefore, the developer not only has to ensure that gestures are quickly and correctly recognized, but also has to provide a guide that allows a rapid and easy learning of these gestures.

The teaching of multi-touch and mid-air gestures is more difficult than that of single-touch gestures. In the case of the latter, the hand posture is irrelevant - users only need to follow a path correctly to perform a command. But with an extension to multi-touch and mid-air gestures, the position and movement of several fingers or even the whole hand becomes relevant. Teaching systems usually instruct the user about the necessary hand movement and path for a gesture rather than the posture and form of contact, focusing on commands that can also be performed with a single-touch input device like a mouse or a pen. (Freeman et al., 2009)

3.1 Discoverability

A disadvantage with gestures, as already identified by Baudel and Beaudouin-Lafon in 1993, is the fact that they are neither self-revealing nor self-explanatory. A named button on a toolbar has an explicit purpose and is also easy to find, gestures, however, may be arbitrary and are usually more difficult to discover.

In order to solve this problem, Bau and Mackay (2008) proposed *OctoPocus*, a dynamic guide that combines feedforward and feedback mechanisms. After a press-and-wait

4

gesture, a map of all possible gestures, visualized through coloured templates, is displayed around the current cursor position. As the user begins to follow a path, the other paths become progressively thinner, indicating that they're less likely to be recognized, until they disappear (see Figure 1).

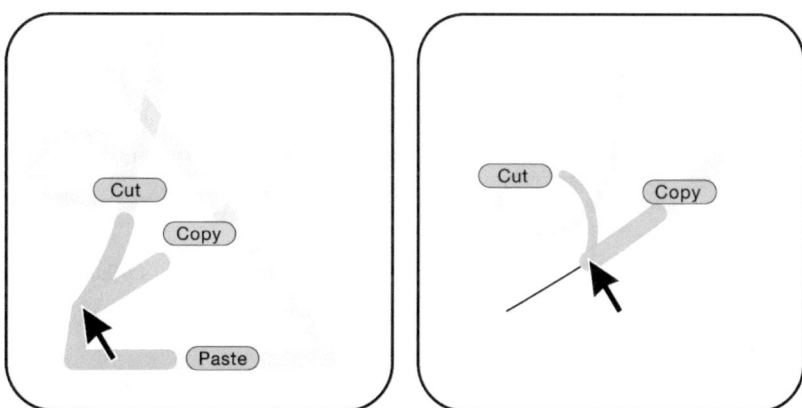

Figure 1: The possible gestures Cut, Copy and Paste are displayed around the current cursor position, visualized as coloured paths with bolder prefixes. As the user begins to follow a path, the prefixes move accordingly and commands that differ too much from the current path become thinner (Cut) or even disappear (Paste). (Bau & Mackay, 2008)

A solution that is also suitable for multi-touch input is the *ShadowGuides* system by Freeman et al. A so-called user-shadow visualizes the user's input, giving feedback on what parts of the hand are in contact with the surface. The user shadow annotations demonstrate possible gestures available from the current hand pose, the registration pose guide informs the user about alternative registration poses. (2009)

Another, a little different approach is *GestureBar* by Bragdon et al. While the aforementioned learning guides employ the "learning-by-doing" technique, *GestureBar* separates the learning area from the user's document and discloses information about a gesture only if needed. The system works like a traditional toolbar - the user can click an item to find details about the execution of the command and to test it in an experimental area. (Bragdon, Zeleznik, Williamson, Miller & LaViola, 2009)

3.2 Memorability

While conventional commands only have to be recognized, gestures need to be known and remembered before executing them (Bau & Mackay, 2008).

One possibility to create memorable gestures is to make them as intuitive as possible, as they are more likely to be remembered that way (Wachs, Kölsch, Stern & Edan, 2011). Wobbrock et al. researched these natural gestures and found that although there are common features used by nearly all of the participants, gestures are far from being "obvious" and that it is difficult to design a gesture set that feels natural for every user. People often used reversible gestures to achieve two opposing effects and used more fingers for moving larger objects, mirroring their experiences in the real world. They were also strongly influenced by their knowledge of traditional computers, using gestures that could also be performed with a mouse (even tapping their fingers as if clicking it) and locating the "Close" gesture at the top-right corner of objects as if they were using a Windows PC. (2009)

Another aspect to remember is the fact that the concept of intuitiveness strongly depends on culture and experience. Many mid-air gestures used in everyday life strongly differ from country to country - a nod, for example, will be commonly interpreted as an indication of agreement, but there are some countries, like Greece for instance, where it stands for the exact opposite. Another example is the pinch-to-zoom gesture that will come natural to every regular smartphone user, but not to someone who has never seen a touchscreen.

An alternative to intuitive gestures are the so-called Marking Menus that combine named commands in a pie menu and gestures. That way, they ease the transition from novice- to expert-mode usage. A further development of Marking Menus are the *Augmented Letters* by Roy et al., where the user activates a pie menu by drawing the letter the elements start with. After that, he can choose from the menu by extending the gesture (see Figure 2). (Roy, Malacria, Guiard, Lecolinet & Eagan, 2013)

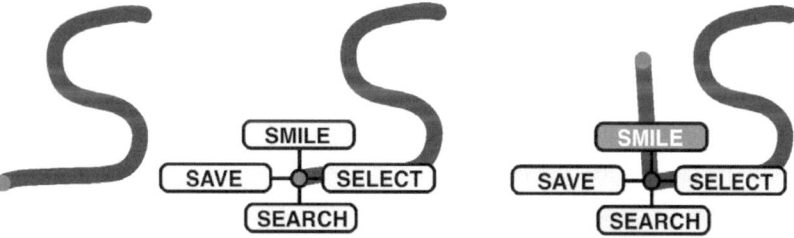

Figure 2: The functionality of *Augmented Letters*: The user already knows that his desired command (Smile) starts with an S. Therefore, he draws the letter and invokes a menu of which he can choose the correct command by appending a tail stroke upwards. (Roy et al., 2013)

3.3 Fatigue

Gestures normally involve more muscles than other interaction techniques (Baudel & Beaudouin-Lafon, 1993), and especially mid-air gestures, but also gestures that require muscle tension and complex movements over a long period of time can be very exhausting. Therefore, developers should design gestures that are quick and comfortable to execute.

One approach are the so-called *Microgestures* - tiny gestures that can even be executed during other activities and therefore allow true multitasking. A possible area of usage is driving, where small tasks like changing the volume of the radio can thus be performed without the potential risk of releasing the steering wheel. This idea has of course been already partially implemented with the integration of additional control elements in the steering wheel. But microinteractions could also be incorporated in other fields of our everyday life, like when writing with a pen or holding a cash card. (Wolf, 2011)

Another aspect, addressed by Forlines and others that needs to be considered is the fact that many bimanual interactions in the real world are asymmetric, with the non-dominant hand being slower and less precise than the dominant hand. Therefore, gestures need to be equally easy for left- and right-handed users and should not demand too much of a person's non-dominant hand. (Forlines, Wigdor, Shen & Balakrishnan, 2007)

3.4 Recognition Errors

With gesture-based interaction, recognition errors are almost inevitable since the user's intention is – unlike with buttons and menus – not explicit (Arvo&Novins, 2006). As a consequence, the system should provide sufficient feedback as well as a general „undo" option (Fourney, 2010). The aforementioned *OctoPocus*, for example, provides feedback by changing the thickness of the path indicating the probability of a correct recognition.

3.4.1 Immersion

Among the recognition errors is the immersion or Midas Touch problem. It describes the fact that every hand movement can be interpreted by the system as a gesture, whether it was intended or not. Baudel and Beaudouin-Lafon already identified the immersion problem in 1993 and reacted by defining a limited Interaction Zone in their gesture-based presentation system *Charade*.

3.4.2 Exit errors

Another recognition error, or rather a special case of the immersion problem is the exit error, described by Tuddenham et al.: Users are having problems breaking contact with an interactive surface without evoking some kind of change in the system. Since the shape of the hand's contact with the surface changes as it is lifted, simply removing it may cause modification, especially with highly sensitive systems. (Tuddenham, Kirk & Izadi, 2010)

4. Conclusion

Gesture-based interaction can be a very efficient and enjoyable form of input, but the need to learn and to remember the gestures may present a barrier especially for unexperienced and infrequent users (Bau & Mackay, 2008; Freeman et al., 2009). Therefore, novice users need support in learning the available gesture sets. Marking menus or the *AugmentedLetters* mentioned in Section 3.2 seem like a good solution since they ease the transition from reading commands to blindly executing a gesture and thus from novice to expert usage.

With the increasing prevalence of smartphones, touchscreen computers and public displays, gesture-based input becomes more and more relevant. However, we still do not exploit the full potentialities of gestures, and are very much under the influence of the desktop paradigm, so who knows what possibilities are to come if gestural input truly arrives in our everyday life.

References:

J. Arvo and K. Novins. Fluid sketching of directed graphs. In *Proceedings of the 7th Australasian User Interface Conference - Volume 50, AUIC '06*, pages 81–86, Darlinghurst, Australia, 2006. Australian Computer Society, Inc.

O. Bau and W. E. Mackay. Octopocus: A dynamic guide for learning gesture-based command sets. In *Proceedings of the 21st Annual ACM Symposium on User Interface Software and Technology, UIST '08*, pages 37–46, New York, NY, USA, 2008. ACM.

T. Baudel and M. Beaudouin-Lafon. *Charade: Remote control of objects using free-hand gestures*. Commun. ACM, 36(7):28–35, July 1993.

A. Bellucci, A. Malizia, and I. Aedo. *Light on horizontal interactive surfaces: Input space for tabletop computing*. ACM Comput. Surv., 46(3):32:1–32:42, Jan. 2014.

A. Bragdon, R. Zeleznik, B. Williamson, T. Miller, and J. J. LaViola, Jr. Gesturebar: Improving the approachability of gesture-based interfaces. In *Proceedings of the SIGCHI Conference on Human Factors in Computing Systems, CHI '09*, pages 2269–2278, New York, NY, USA, 2009. ACM.

P. Brandl, C. Forlines, D. Wigdor, M. Haller, and C. Shen. Combining and measuring the benefits of bimanual pen and direct-touch interaction on horizontal interfaces. In *Proceedings of the Working Conference on Advanced Visual Interfaces, AVI '08*, pages 154–161, New York, NY, USA, 2008. ACM.

X. Cao, E. Ofek, and D. Vronay. Evaluation of alternative presentation control techniques. In *CHI '05 Extended Abstracts on Human Factors in Computing Systems, CHI EA '05*, pages 1248–1251, New York, NY, USA, 2005. ACM.

C. Forlines, D. Wigdor, C. Shen, and R. Balakrishnan. Direct-touch vs. mouse input for tabletop displays. In *Proceedings of the SIGCHI Conference on Human Factors in Computing Systems, CHI '07*, pages 647–656, New York, NY, USA, 2007. ACM.

A. Fourney, M. Terry, and R. Mann. Gesturing in the wild: Understanding the effects and implications of gesture-based interaction for dynamic presentations. In *Proceedings of the 24th BCS Interaction Specialist Group Conference, BCS '10*, pages 230–240, Swinton, UK, UK, 2010. British Computer Society.

D. Freeman, H. Benko, M. R. Morris, and D. Wigdor. Shadowguides: Visualizations for in-situ learning of multi-touch and whole-hand gestures. In *Proceedings of the ACM International Conference on Interactive Tabletops and Surfaces, ITS '09*, pages 165–172, New York, NY, USA, 2009. ACM.

Q. Roy, S. Malacria, Y. Guiard, E. Lecolinet, and J. Eagan. Augmented letters: Mnemonic gesture-based shortcuts. In *Proceedings of the SIGCHI Conference on Human Factors in Computing Systems, CHI '13*, pages 2325–2328, New York, NY, USA, 2013. ACM.

P. Tuddenham, D. Kirk, and S. Izadi. Graspables revisited: Multi-touch vs. tangible input for tabletop displays in acquisition and manipulation tasks. In *Proceedings of the SIGCHI Conference on Human Factors in Computing Systems, CHI '10,* pages 2223–2232, New York, NY, USA, 2010. ACM.

J. P. Wachs, M. Kölsch, H. Stern, and Y. Edan. *Vision-based hand-gesture applications.* Commun. ACM, 54(2):60–71, Feb. 2011.

D. Watson, M. Hancock, R. L. Mandryk, and M. Birk. Deconstructing the touch experience. In *Proceedings of the 2013 ACM International Conference on Interactive Tabletops and Surfaces, ITS '13,* pages 199–208, New York, NY, USA, 2013. ACM.

J. O. Wobbrock, M. R. Morris, and A. D. Wilson. User-defined gestures for surface computing. In *Proceedings of the SIGCHI Conference on Human Factors in Computing Systems, CHI '09,* pages 1083–1092, New York, NY, USA, 2009. ACM.

K. Wolf. Microinteractions for supporting grasp tasks through usage of spare attentional and motor resources. In *Proceedings of the 29th Annual European Conference on Cognitive Ergonomics, ECCE '11,* pages 221–224, New York, NY, USA, 2011. ACM.

YOUR KNOWLEDGE HAS VALUE

- We will publish your bachelor's and master's thesis, essays and papers

- Your own eBook and book - sold worldwide in all relevant shops

- Earn money with each sale

Upload your text at www.GRIN.com
and publish for free